This book belongs to

Fes

TEDDY

This book is dedicated to my children - Mikey, Kobe, and Jojo.
Life is full of choices. Choose to be happy, not grumpy.

Grumpy Ninja

Pictures by
Jelena Stupar

By Mary Nhin

Grumpy Ninja was the grumpiest ninja you'll ever meet.
For breakfast, his mom made his sister's favorite dish.

This made him grumpy.

When Grumpy Ninja got to school late,
it made him super grumpy.

During class, he couldn't get the pencil sharpener to work.

After school, his friends decided to head to the beach and Grumpy Ninja tagged along.

Positive and Earth Ninja grabbed his hands to pull him by the water, but Grumpy NInja wasn't happy about it.

Before you knew it, Grumpy Ninja was splashing around and having a blast! And then, he felt something he had never felt before. What was that feeling?

Ahhhh. Happiness.

"How can I have more of that?" he asked as if one could bottle up happiness and buy it. Positive Ninja smiled and replied, "We can't buy it, but we can cultivate it. I'll show you."

Instead of focusing on what's wrong, we can choose to focus on what's right. For example, we have all five fingers on our hand. This helps us draw and write.

We have ears to listen to music. Believe it or not, some people can't hear with their ears.

We have two legs that help us do flips.
And two feet that help us kick.

We have a home where we can take bubble baths.

If we take time to pray or meditate, it will help us have gratitude for the small things in life.

Like sunshine and the food we eat.

The air we breathe and the clean water we drink.

We can be thankful for birds and bees and flowers and trees.

And, most of all, our family.

Just a simple change of perspective and a bit of gratitude are all you need as your secret weapons to banish grumpiness.

Sign up for new Ninja book releases at GrowGrit.co

 @marynhin   @GrowGrit
#NinjaLifeHacks

 Mary Nhin   Grow Grit

▶ Grow Grit

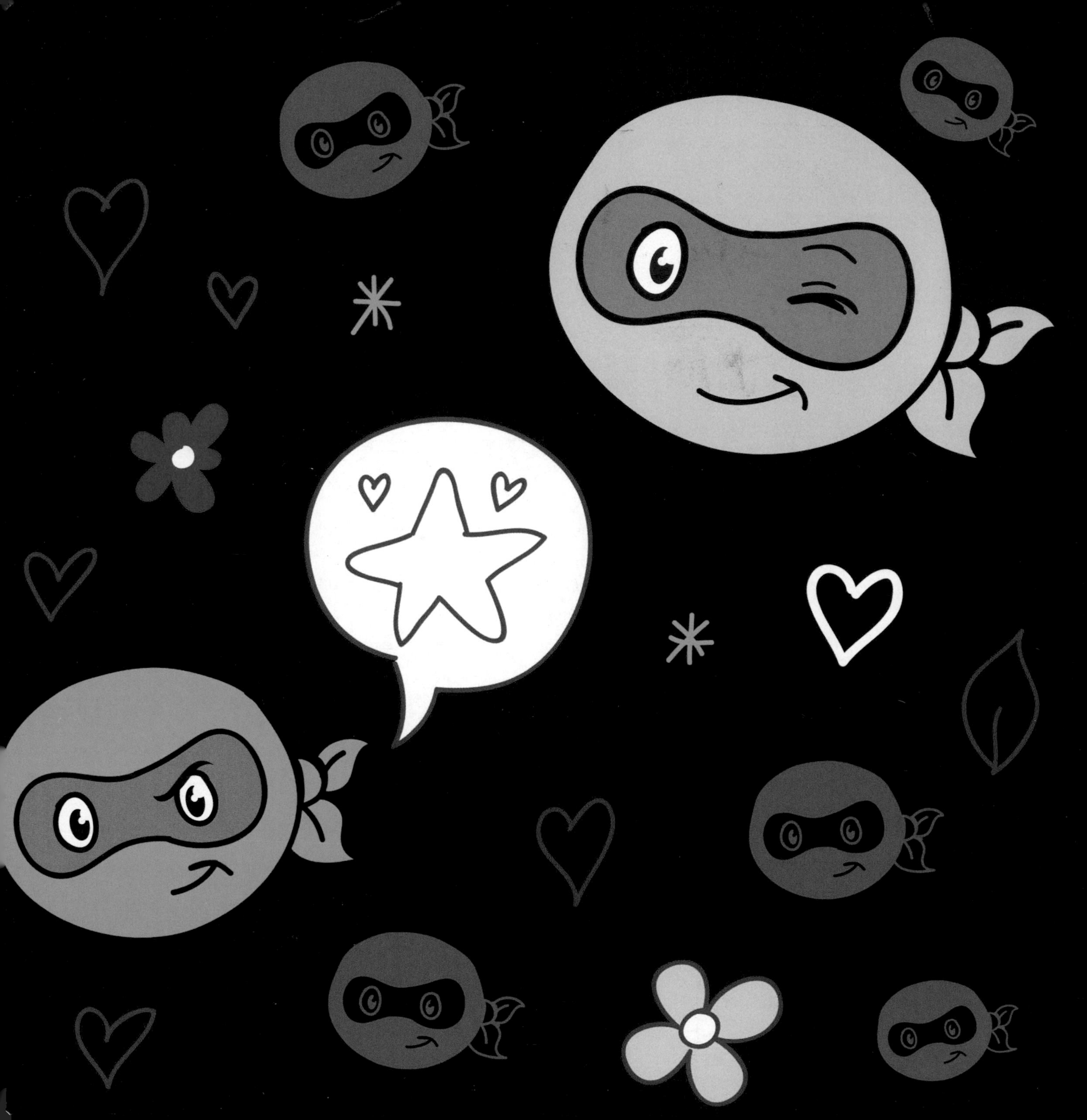

Made in the USA
Columbia, SC
04 August 2020